The Bachelor's Cookbook

by
Gil, Rees, & Mark
Gibson

August, 1985   10,000 books

Additional copies may be obtained from
The Bachelor's Cookbook
P.O. Box 117
Waycross, GA 31502

Cover Design by Marta Shattuck

Photographs by David Johnston - Waycross, GA

ISBN - 0-941162-03-6

Printed in the United States of America
by
Moran Printing Company
Orlando, Florida

ATTENTION ALL NEW COOKS

First, if we can cook these recipes so can you! They are easy and written step by step.

Cooking can really be fun. Start with some simple recipes. Use package mixes with little preparation and gradually move into the recipes with several ingredients and steps to follow.

Have the basics on hand. Take time to stock the most common items. We have made a list on the next page. It can be expensive stocking the cupboard and pantry the first time so if you live near home scarf some from your mom.

When planning a meal for company try and have as much done before hand as possible. If you are cooking the meat on the grill just before serving, have vegetable and salad that can be prepared ahead.

The "no fun" part of cooking is the cleaning up afterwards. The mess won't go away on its own - so just go ahead and clean the kitchen. It won't hurt you and if you do it after every meal, it sure is easier - take our word for it.

Just think — Your mother will be so happy you are eating better. Your girl friend will be thrilled you can cook a meal for her. Your wallet will be delighted because you are saving money.

KITCHEN BASICS

In Refrigerator

Mayonnaise
Pickle relish
Eggs
Milk
Mustard
Catsup
Parmesan cheese
Margarine or butter
Jelly
Italian salad dressing
Concentrated lemon
  juice
Bacon bits

Freezer

Chopped onions
Cool Whip

Shelf Near Stove

Salt
Pepper
Cooking oil
Baking soda
Worcestershire sauce
Vinegar
Vanilla
Tabasco sauce
Garlic powder
Cinnamon, ground
Soy sauce
Meat tenderizer
Salad seasoning

Pantry

Sugar
Flour
Rice
Cream of chicken
  soup
Cream of
  mushroom soup
Cream of tomato
  soup
Cheddar cheese
  soup
Dry onion soup mix
Shortening
Bisquick
Bread
Peanut butter

NICE TO HAVE ON HAND FOR UNPLANNED MEALS

Spaghetti noodles
Jar of spaghetti sauce
Pancake syrup
Jello
Canned tuna fish
Dried chip beef
Chunky beef and vegetable soup
Canned baked beans

MEASUREMENTS

3 teaspoons   = 1 tablespoon   1 stick margarine = ½ cup
2 tablespoons = 1 ounce   1 stick margarine = 8 tablespoons
4 tablespoons = ¼ cup   1 stick margarine = 4 ounces
8 tablespoons = ½ cup   1 stick margarine = ¼ pound

```
 1 cup  =    8 ounces = ½ pint
 2 cups =   16 ounces = 1 pint
 4 cups =   32 ounces = 2 pints = 1 quart
 8 cups =   64 ounces = 4 pints = 2 quarts = ½ gallon
16 cups = 128 ounces = 8 pints = 4 quarts = 1 gallon
```

Be sure to use measuring cups for exact measurements.
   Not a coffee cup.
Measuring spoons are a big help. They come in ⅛ teaspoon, ¼ teaspoon, ½ teaspoon, 1 teaspoon, and 1 tablespoon.

Salad   Dinner   Knife Teaspoon
Fork   Fork
                   Tablespoon
                       or
                  Serving Spoon
                  (placed beside
                  dish to be served)

5

CONTENTS

Appetizers 9

Salads 15

Breads 21

Quick & Easy Meals 27

Meats 43

Vegetables 63

Desserts 77

Index 93

Appetizers

APPETIZERS

Barbeque Bean Dip 10
Chili Dip 9
Cocktail Sauce for Shrimp or Oysters 12
Deviled Ham Dip 11
Dill Dip 10
Easy Guacamole 11
Fancy Dogs 10
Oyster Dip 9
Salmon Spread 11
Shrimp or Oyster Cocktails 12

OYSTER DIP
"Super! Our friends love it!"

1 3½ ounce can of smoked oysters
½ pint sour cream (8 ounces)

Worcestershire sauce
Tabasco sauce
Salt

1. Drain oysters and chop into very small pieces.
2. Stir in sour cream. Add salt and Worcestershire sauce to taste. (1 or 2 teaspoons of sauce) Add a couple drops of Tabasco sauce -depending on how hot you like it.
3. Mix well and place in refrigerator.

Needs to be made several hours ahead for flavor. Serve with potato chips. A favorite!!

CHILI DIP

1 15 ounce can chili (without beans)

1 8 ounce package cream cheese

1. Place chili in sauce pan over low heat.
2. Break cream cheese into small pieces and add. Heat until all cheese is melted and mixed.
3. Serve with corn chips or nachos.

ONION DIP

1 package dry onion soup mix

1 pint sour cream (16 ounces)

Use 1 envelope (they come two to a box) of onion soup.

1. Combine dry soup mix and sour cream. Mix well.
2. Place in refrigerator until ready to serve. This is better prepared several hours early.

BARBEQUE BEAN DIP

½ cup barbeque sauce (any brand)

1 13 ounce can bean and bacon soup

1. Combine soup and barbeque sauce mixing well.
2. Serve with potato chips or corn chips.

DILL DIP

1 cup mayonnaise
½ pint sour cream (8 ounces)
1½ tablespoon dried dill

1½ teaspoon Worcestershire sauce
1½ teaspoon onion powder

1. Combine all the ingredients in a bowl.
2. Stir to mix well and then refrigerate until ready to serve.
3. Serve with potato chips.

FANCY DOGS

1 can refrigerator biscuits

1 package weiners

1. Turn oven on to 400 degrees to preheat.
2. Cut as many weiners as needed in half, crosswise.
3. Open can of biscuits, cut each one in half and flatten by pressing out on waxed paper or by pressing and spreading with hands.
4. Roll each weiner half in flattened biscuit dough.
5. Bake at 400 or 425 for 10 minutes. Check directions on your particular brand of biscuits.

EASY GUACAMOLE

3 avocados
½ teaspoon garlic salt

1 tablespoon lemon juice
2 to 3 tablespoons mayonnaise

1. Peel avocados, remove seeds and mash with a fork.
2. Add lemon juice, garlic, salt, and mayonnaise.
3. Refrigerate until serving. Serve with chips or crackers.

SALMON SPREAD

1 15 ounce can salmon
1 8 ounce package cream
   cheese
1 teaspoon horseradish

¼ to ½ teaspoon salt
1 small onion chopped or ½
   cup frozen chopped onion
   thawed and drained well

1. Remove bones from salmon and discard.
2. Mix all ingredients together and place in a small, shallow bowl or
   mold and chill in refrigerator for an hour or so.
3. Turn out on to a plate by running knife around the sides to help
   release it from bowl.

This will set and take on the shape of the container. It is a spread to
be served with crackers.

DEVILED HAM DIP

1 12 ounce carton cottage
   cheese (cream style)

1 2½ ounce can deviled ham
½ envelope dry onion soup mix

1. Combine cheese, ham and onion soup mix and mix well.
2. Prepare ahead and let set in refrigerator an hour. Serve with
   potato chips.

COCKTAIL SAUCE FOR SHRIMP OR OYSTERS

1 cup catsup
2 teaspoons horseradish (or
      more)

1 teaspoon Worcestershire

1. Mix ingredients together.
2. Taste. You can add more horseradish and make it as hot or biting as you like. This is super for boiled shrimp, raw or roasted oysters.

SHRIMP OR OYSTER COCKTAILS

Put a little lettuce in a dish, a few boiled and peeled shrimp or raw oysters, add several spoonfuls of cocktail sauce and you have a fancy shrimp cocktail or oyster cocktail.

Salads

SALADS

Banana Salad 17
Congealed Fruit Salad 15
Cranberry Salad 18
Lettuce Wedges 16
Peach Salad 17
Pear Salad 17
Pineapple Salad 17
Quick Aspic Salad 18
Tossed Green Salad 15
Tuna Fish Salad 16

TOSSED GREEN SALAD

Lettuce	Cucumbers
Tomato	Bean sprouts
Onion	Boiled eggs
Carrot	Croutons
Green bellpepper	Bacon bits
Green olives	And whatever
Ripe olives	Salt and pepper

You can use as many different things in a salad as you want. You start with your lettuce and add any or all. First remove the lettuce stem by hitting it on the sink. It will break loose and can easily be pulled out. Remove limp outer leaves and discard. Wash under running water. Shake off as much of the water as you can. Break open and set out to drain a little. Break in small pieces into large salad bowl. Make the pieces small enough for easy eating. Now be creative and add what you like.

Pour an Italian dressing over it, toss and let it set and wilt 30 minutes to an hour.

CONGEALED FRUIT SALAD

1 15 ounce can fruit cocktail	1 cup of water
1 3½ ounce package cherry Jello	½ cup of drained syrup from fruit

1. Drain fruit and save juice.
2. Combine 1 cup water and ½ cup of juice in sauce pan and bring to a boil.
3. Add Jello mix and stir until dissolved.
4. Pour liquid over fruit in 8 x 8 dish or individual cups. Refrigerate several hours until firm.

Jello packages call for 2 cups of water. When adding fruit it is best to omit ½ cup of liquid to allow for liquid in fruit.

TUNA FISH SALAD
"A salad or sandwich"

1 6 ounce can tuna	2 tablespoons mayonnaise
2 hard boiled eggs, chopped	1 tablespoon sweet pickle relish

1. Drain oil liquid from tuna fish. We use tuna canned in spring water and you have no oily taste.
2. Break tuna into small pieces, add mayonnaise, pickles, and chopped eggs and mix.
3. Serve on lettuce leaves as a salad lunch or on bread spread with mayonnaise as sandwich.

Serves 2

If you have regular tuna canned in oil and don't care for the strong oily taste you can run hot or boiling water over it in a strainer, drain or squeeze out water — gets rid of the strong taste.

LETTUCE WEDGES

1 head of lettuce	Thousand Island or French dressing

1. Wash lettuce, remove stem, and drain.
2. Cut lettuce into 6 wedges.
3. Place wedge on salad plate and pour several tablespoons of dressing over it.

QUICK FRUIT SALADS
No Cooking

BANANA SALAD

Banana   **Mayonnaise**
Lettuce

1. Peel banana and cut in half lengthwise and then across.
2. Place two quarters on lettuce leaf, add one half teaspoon mayonnaise. Ready to serve.
3. You can add a cherry or ground peanuts to top of mayonnaise for garnish.

PEACH SALAD

1 can peach halves   **Lettuce**
Cottage cheese

1. Drain peaches.
2. Place peach half on lettuce leaf. Fill center with cottage cheese.

PEAR SALAD

1 can pear halves   **Lettuce**
Cream cheese

1. Drain pears.
2. Set cream cheese out to soften. Spread layer of cheese on cut side of pear half.
3. Place cheese side down on lettuce leaf.

PINEAPPLE SALAD

1 can pineapple slices   **Lettuce**
Cottage cheese

1. Drain pineapple slices.
2. Place on lettuce leaf and top with scoop of cottage cheese.

CRANBERRY SALAD

1 3½ ounce package cherry
  Jello
1 cup hot water
½ cup chopped nuts

1 8 ounce can crushed
  pineapple
1 16 ounce can whole
  cranberry sauce (be sure
  you have whole berries)

1. Dissolve Jello in boiling water.
2. Drain pineapple well. (The best way is to squeeze out the liquid in your hand).
3. Add pineapple, cranberry sauce and nuts to Jello and mix well.
4. Pour into square casserole dish or individual salad cups. Chill.

QUICK ASPIC SALAD

1 15 ounce can stewed
  tomatoes
1 3 ounce box strawberry Jello

2 to 3 tablespoons tarragon
  vinegar

1. Heat tomatoes in small sauce pan.
2. Add dry Jello and vinegar, stir to make sure Jello has dissolved.
3. Pour into dish and refrigerate.

Be sure and get stewed tomatoes not just regular canned ones.

Breads

BREADS

Beer Muffins 23
Biscuits 23
Brown & Serve Rolls 21
Buttered Bread Slices 21
Canned Refrigerator Rolls and Biscuits 21
Cheese Toast. 22
Cinnamon Toast 22
Garlic Bread 22
Grandmother's Popovers 24
Package Muffins. 21
Real Biscuits 24
2 Man-Size Biscuits 23

HOT BREAD

Adds **so** much to a meal. Here are 4 ultra-easy suggestions.

1. Hot Buttered Bread slices

2. Brown & Serve Rolls

3. Canned Refrigerator Rolls & Biscuits

4. Packaged Muffin Mixes

1. BUTTERED BREAD SLICES

"This is the bottom rung on the ladder of hot bread" but it's good. Spread 2 or 3 slices of bread with butter, wrap in foil and place in 325 to 350 degree oven while you are preparing dinner. 10 to 15 minutes.

2. BROWN & SERVE ROLLS

Come in a metal pan ready to slide in oven and heat. Biscuits and all type rolls found in bread section of store.

3. CANNED REFRIGERATOR ROLLS AND BISCUITS

Just preheat your oven to 400 degrees or temperature suggested on package. Break open tube, separate and place on flat sheet pan and bake 8 to 10 minutes. Easy - Easy - but adds so much to a meal. Look for them in the dairy section with milk and cheeses.

4. PACKAGE MUFFINS

There are any number of package muffin mixes, Blueberry, Honey & Dates, Bran, Banana. Easy, Easy. Try a package - You only need a muffin pan (you can use paper muffin liners if you do not want to grease and clean the pan). Add egg, milk or water, stir, spoon into pan and bake usually 10 to 15 minutes.

5. HOMEMADE

CINNAMON TOAST

Bread   **Ground cinnamon**
Sugar   **Margarine**

1. In small dish mix 2 or 3 tablespoons of sugar with ½ teaspoon of cinnamon.
2. Spread soft margarine thickly on bread.
3. Sprinkle sugar mixture evenly on top.
4. Place on flat pan or foil on top shelf of electric oven and bottom shelf under flames in gas oven. Broil on 400 degrees until bubbly and bread edges begin to brown.

CHEESE TOAST

Bread   **American cheese, slices**

1. Place 1 slice of cheese on each piece of bread.
2. Place on flat pan (on top shelf of electric oven and bottom shelf under flames for gas oven) at 400 degrees on broil.

   Watch carefully. All you want to do is melt cheese. It will brown slightly - but watch - it will burn fast!

GARLIC BREAD

Bread or buns   **1 teaspoon garlic powder**
½ stick margarine

You can use hotdog buns, hamburger buns, English muffins or French bead.

1. Soften margarine, and add garlic powder.
2. Place bread, crust side down on baking pan. Spread margarine over cut side of bread.
3. Place on top shelf of electric oven and set on broil. Place on bottom shelf of gas oven under flame. Broil for 1 to 2 minutes.

   You will need to watch it because it will start to brown fast and burn easily. If using French bread first toast one side slightly - turn and spread unbaked side with margarine then broil.

BEER MUFFINS

2 cups Bisquick   6 ounces of beer
1 to 2 tablespoons sugar

1. First turn oven on to 450 degrees so it will be preheated.
2. Be sure to rub inside of each muffin cup with liquid vegetable oil or margarine so muffins will not stick to pan.
3. Combine Bisquick and sugar and then stir in beer.
4. Put into greased muffin pan filling each about half full.
5. Bake at 450 degrees for 10 minutes.

2 MAN-SIZE BISCUITS

1 cup Bisquick   4 tablespoons milk
1 teaspoon vinegar

1. Turn oven on to 450 degrees. Put Bisquick in small bowl.
2. Combine vinegar and milk, stir into Bisquick - mix fast - batter will be sticky.
3. Divide into 2 large biscuits - just pat them down on a pan with fingers.
4. Bake 5 to 6 minutes.

Can be cut in half and make 1 man-size biscuit.

BISCUITS
Using Biscuit Mix

2 cups Bisquick   ½ cup milk

1. Turn oven on to 400 degrees to preheat.
2. Measure dry mix into bowl, slowly add milk, mixing as you add.
3. Place waxed paper on counter top, sprinkle with some of dry mix.
4. Turn dough out on to paper. Pat out to desired thickness around ¼ to ½ inch.
5. Cut circles with a glass, snuff can, or other round object (Dip into flour or mix to prevent dough from sticking to it).
6. Place on ungreased flat pan and bake 8 to 10 minutes.

REAL BISCUITS

2 **cups self rising flour**
¾ **cup milk**

¾ **cup solid shortening (comes in can, looks like lard; example - Crisco)**

1. Turn oven on to 400 degrees to preheat.
2. Measure flour into large bowl.
3. Cut shortening into flour.* See below.
4. Add milk, mixing as you add.
5. Spread waxed paper or plastic wrap on counter top and sprinkle it with flour. Turn dough out on floured surface and pat or roll out to desired thickness, anywhere from ¼ to ½ inch depending if you like thick or thin. If dough is a little sticky and hard to handle add a little more flour and mix it in well. We pat it out thin because we like real thin biscuits.
6. Cut circles with water glass, jar, snuff can, or any round object, the size you like. Dip cutter in flour to prevent sticking.
7. Place on flat pan and bake at 400 degrees for 10 minutes.

* This just means to get that big lump of solid shortening mixed as evenly as possible through the flour. You can use 2 knives, slicing through flour, a fork and mash it into the flour, or use your hands. Slice, mash, or squeeze but mix it into flour until shortening is in pieces the size of peas.

GRANDMOTHER'S POPOVERS

2 **eggs**
1 **cup milk**

1 **cup sifted flour**
½ **teaspoon salt**

1. Grease muffin tins well with oil, margarine, or use non-stick spray. Just take some on your fingers and smear it in each cup - or muffins will stick.
2. Beat eggs in a medium size bowl.
3. Add milk, flour and salt. Mix well with a spoon, (disregard the lumps).
4. Fill muffin tins ¾ full. Put into a COLD oven. Set oven for 450 degrees and bake 30 minutes.

   The secret is starting with a cold oven. Yield 8 large muffins or 15 small.

Quick & Easy Meals

QUICK AND EASY MEALS

Cheeseburgers 28
Corned Beef Hash and Eggs 31
Cream Chip Beef on Toast 31
Creamed Tuna on Toast 30
Crustless Quiche 34
French Toast 32
Hamburgers Deluxe 27
Instant Stew 30
Mushroom Burger 28
Old Fashioned Hamburgers 28
Omelettes 35
Onion Burger 29
Pancakes 32
Pizza Burger 29
Plain Hamburgers 27
Quick Pizza's 29

EGGS
Deviled Eggs 38
Eggs and Cheese 36
Fried Egg 37
Fried Rice 37
Hard Boiled Eggs 38
Sausage and Eggs 36
Scrambled Eggs 36

SANDWICHES
Bacon, Lettuce, and Tomato 40
Deviled Ham Sandwiches 39
Egg McSandwich 40
Egg Salad Sandwiches 40
Fancy Hotdogs 39
Grilled Cheese Sandwiches 39
Tuna Fish Salad Sandwich 40

PLAIN HAMBURGERS

1 pound ground meat   **½ to 1 teaspoon salt**

1. Mix salt into meat.
2. Mold meat into 5 patties or 4 large ones.
3. Place in hot frying pan. (Most ground meat has enough fat in it to prevent it from sticking.) If you are not sure just go ahead and spray pan with non-stick spray or melt a teaspoon or two or margarine in pan before putting in hamburgers.
4. Fry on medium heat 5 to 7 minutes on each side.

Turn your hamburger only once. Naturally, thick burgers will take longer to cook than thin ones. Cut one and see if it is the way you like it. Soon you will be able to judge easily.

To Broil

Turn oven to broil which means in an electric oven only the top unit is on. Raise top shelf so that it is in the top of oven usually 4 to 6 inches from top unit. Use a broiler pan with a rack so that grease will drip into pan below the rack and the burgers. Broil 6 to 8 minutes on each side. For gas stove place at bottom of oven under flames for broiling.

HAMBURGERS DELUXE
"Our Favorite - Super Moist & Tasty"

1 pound ground meat   **½ cup steak sauce**
2 tablespoons Worcestershire   **½ to 1 teaspoon salt**
   sauce   **⅛ teaspoon pepper**

1. Combine meat, sauces and seasoning.
2. Make into 4 or 5 patties and cook on top of stove or grill. (See plain Hamburger for cooking directions.)

Makes a super moist tasty burger.

CHEESEBURGERS

Hamburger patties   **Thin cheese slices**

1. See Plain Hamburgers or Deluxe
2. Just before burgers are done lay a slice of cheese on top of each pattie. Cheese will heat and melt slightly. (We use American cheese that comes sliced for sandwiches.)

MUSHROOM BURGER

1 pound ground meat   **2 tablespoons Worcestershire**
¼ to ½ cup steak sauce   **sauce**
½ teaspoon salt   **2 ounce can mushroom slices**

1. Combine meat, salt and sauces.
2. Drain mushrooms and add.
3. Mold into 4 or 5 burgers and pan fry or broil. See Plain Hamburger for cooking directions.

OLD FASHIONED HAMBURGERS

1 pound ground meat   **2 slices of bread**
1 teaspoon salt

1. Place bread in water until soggy.
2. Squeeze out most of water and combine bread with meat - add salt, mixing as evenly as possible.
3. Mold into 4 to 5 patties and fry.

   This makes for moister hamburgers. See Plain Hamburgers for cooking directions.

ONION BURGER

1 pound ground meat
½ envelope dry onion soup
 mix

1 to 2 tablespoons water

1. Combine meat, dry soup mix and water.
2. Mold into 4 or 5 patties.
3. Place in lightly greased frying pan and cook over medium high heat 5 to 7 minutes per side.
4. See Plain Hamburger for cooking directions.

PIZZA BURGER

1 pound ground meat
½ to 1 teaspoon salt
½ teaspoon pepper

½ cup pizza sauce
Mozzarella cheese

1. Combine ground meat with salt, pepper and ½ of the pizza sauce.
2. Mold into 4 or 5 patties.
3. Place burgers in heated frying pan. Just before burgers are done put a spoonful of sauce on top of each burger and a slice of cheese. See Plain Burger for cooking directions.

QUICK PIZZA'S

English muffins or hamburger
 buns
1 jar of pizza sauce

Ground beef, sausage, or
 whatever you like
Mozzarella cheese

1. Turn oven on to 350 degrees.
2. Brown meat in frying pan on top of stove.
3. Split buns, spoon sauce on each half, sprinkle with grated cheese, and browned meat.
4. Place in oven for 10 minutes - watch.

INSTANT STEW

1 19 ounce can thick beef and vegetable soup (the kind that does not need water added)

1 cup instant rice
½ teaspoon salt
1 cup water

1. Put water and salt in a saucepan and bring to a boil.
2. Add instant rice. Cover pan, remove from heat, and let stand 10 minutes.
3. Pour can of thick, ready to serve soup into a pan and heat.
4. Put rice on plates and spoon soup over top.

A great meal when you do not have time to really cook.

Serves 2 or 1 famished mortal

CREAMED TUNA ON TOAST

1 6½ ounce can tuna fish
2 eggs - hard boiled
2 tablespoons flour

2 tablespoons margarine
1 cup milk
Toast

1. Melt margarine in sauce pan over medium to medium high heat.
2. Add flour and mix. This will turn into a paste.
3. Slowly add milk stirring constantly. Continue stirring and cooking until a creamy white sauce is obtained.
4. Drain tuna and break into small pieces and add. Add chopped boiled eggs.

Ready to serve over toast. Great lunch or supper.

We use tuna canned in water. You can pour hot water over regular tuna to rinse off oil. Then squeeze out extra moisture. This keeps it from tasting strong and oily. Makes all the difference.

CORNED BEEF HASH AND EGGS
"Super breakfast or supper"

1 16 ounce can corned beef hash

3 or 4 poached or sunny side up fried eggs

1. Pat hash down evenly in a flat pan or baking dish. (We use a pie pan.)
2. Place on top shelf of oven that is set on broil at 400 degrees or at bottom of gas oven on broil rack below flames. Broil until top is crisp, usually 10 to 15 minutes.
3. Poach or fry eggs.
4. Serve hash with a spatula or pancake turner so you can lift out a section and place on plate flat with crust still on top. Place egg on top of each serving.

3 to 4 servings

CREAM CHIP BEEF ON TOAST

1 2½ ounce jar dried beef
2 tablespoons margarine

2 tablespoons flour
1 cup milk

1. In a large frying pan melt margarine using medium to medium high heat.
2. Cut or tear beef into small pieces and stir into margarine getting all pieces coated.
3. Add flour and stir.
4. Slowly add milk and continue to stir. A creamy white sauce will form. Cook 2 or 3 minutes stirring continuously. If it is a little too thick add more milk. If it is too thin and runny just cook a little longer. Serve on toast.

Serves 2 to 3

PANCAKES
"Great for Supper as well as Breakfast"

2 cups pancake mix   1 tablespoon oil
1 egg   ¾ cup milk

1. Beat egg in a small bowl and add oil and milk.
2. Add to pancake mix and stir. Don't worry about the lumps. The batter will not be completely smooth.
3. Cook on a hot griddle, or frying pan. Preheat pan and add enough cooking oil to coat bottom.
4. Spoon in batter the size cakes you like. When bubbles form and edges begin to dry, turn. Cook until second side is brown.

Serves 2 to 3

FRENCH TOAST
A great Sunday night supper

1 egg   1 to 2 tablespoons margarine
2 slices bread   Powdered sugar (optional)
1 to 2 tablespoons milk

1. Beat egg and milk together.
2. Melt margarine in frying pan over medium heat. (Just enough to coat bottom of pan.)
3. When pan is hot dip slice of bread into egg, coating both sides. Place in frying pan and cook on both sides until light brown.
4. Place on plate and sprinkle with powdered sugar. Serve with syrup or eat as is. This recipe can easily be doubled or tripled.

Serves 1

Pancakes make a great meal anytime.

CRUSTLESS QUICHE
Broccoli or Spinach

1 10 ounce package frozen
   chopped spinach or
   chopped broccoli
4 eggs
½ cup milk
¼ to ½ cup chopped onion

½ teaspoon pepper
1 cup pitted ripe olives (cut in
   halves)
½ cup grated Parmesan cheese,
   divided
1 tablespoon margarine

1. Chop onion or set out frozen onions to thaw so you can squeeze out extra water due to freezing.
2. Cook spinach or broccoli in 1 cup water for about 6 minutes. Drain well. (We squeeze the spinach in our fist — best way to get the water out.)
3. Beat eggs in a medium size mixing bowl and stir in milk, salt, and pepper and mix.
4. Stir in main vegetable (the broccoli or spinach) and onion, ¼ cup of the Parmesan cheese and olives that have been cut in half.
5. Melt margarine in 8 inch frying pan (medium size one) make sure it coats the bottom and sides so eggs will not stick. Pour in mixture and sprinkle top with remaining ¼ cup cheese.
6. Cover and cook on low heat 15 minutes. Cut into wedges.

Makes 6 nice servings. Serves 3 or 4.

OMELETTES

4 eggs
2 tablespoons margarine
¼ to ½ teaspoon salt

¼ cup (4 tablespoons) milk
Cheese
Other suggestions below

Use small 8 inch or 9 inch frying pan.

1. Melt margarine in pan on medium to medium high heat, tilting it to make sure the bottom and part of sides are coated.
2. Combine eggs, salt, and milk and beat until light and foamy. (you can use handbeater, wire wisk or fork - just beat well.)
3. Pour eggs into heated pan. Do not stir like you would for scrambled eggs - you want this to be one solid piece and look like a fluffy thick egg pancake.
4. As it cooks and begins to set, lift sides with spatula and let uncooked eggs run down to bottom where it will cook faster.
5. Add cheese or vegetables on top and cook for 2 or 3 minutes. You want the sides done but the inside still moist.
6. Carefully slide the spatula under the omelette and fold one half over the other. Continue to cook one-half to one minute. You can place lid on pan and this will help top to cook faster. Serve at once.
Serves 2

Other omelette suggestions - mushrooms, green peppers and onions, canned vegetables, canned vegetable soup not diluted.

SCRAMBLED EGGS

2 eggs   **1 to 2 tablespoons margarine**
2 to 3 tablespoons milk   **Salt**

1. Break eggs into small bowl.
2. Add salt and milk and beat with whisk, fork, or egg beater until well mixed.
3. Put margarine in frying pan and melt on medium to medium high. Spread margarine over entire pan to prevent eggs from sticking.
4. Add beaten eggs and cook until soft and fluffy. Stir while cooking.

SAUSAGE AND EGGS

3 eggs   **¼ pound of ground sausage**
2 or 3 tablespoons milk

1. Brown sausage in frying pan over medium heat. Stir occasionally so that all is browned and broken into small pieces. Be sure sausage is done. Pour off grease.
2. Break eggs into mixing bowl, add milk. Beat with fork, egg beater or whisk.
3. Add to frying pan with sausage and cook until eggs are soft and fluffy, stir while cooking.

Sausage flavor will probably be enough seasoning. We do not add extra salt or pepper because of sausage seasoning. Taste and you can add at table.

EGGS AND CHEESE

1. Follow directions for Scrambled Eggs.
2. When eggs are about done add cheese. This will give it time to melt as eggs continue to cook. It can be grated or cut into small pieces. Continue to stir your eggs and cook as for plain scramble eggs. The cheese just gives an added taste. Good!

FRIED EGG

1 to 2 tablespoons margarine or bacon drippings

**1 egg
Salt and pepper**

1. Heat margarine in small frying pan on medium high.
2. Carefully break egg into pan, salt and pepper.
3. For soft, runny eggs (sunnyside up) spoon the margarine over top. As soon as the white turns "white" and sets remove with spatula.
4. For medium eggs - spoon grease over yolk until it sets or carefully turn egg and cook a few seconds.
5. Well done eggs - turn and let cook until yolk is hard.

Fried egg sandwiches are hard to beat - Fry egg hard and place between bread.

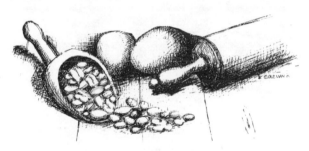

FRIED RICE
"Great Way to use left over rice"

**2 cups cooked rice
3 or 4 strips bacon, fried
2 eggs**

**½ onion or handful of chopped, frozen onions
Soy sauce**

1. Cook rice (see recipe for rice), set aside.
2. Fry bacon in frying pan and remove from grease. Crumble bacon and add to rice.
3. Chop onion and saute' in bacon grease. (Just cook until limp and clear.) When done remove from grease - put with rice and bacon.
4. Scramble the eggs in a little margarine, add rice, bacon, onion and mix all together in frying pan. Add soy sauce to your taste.

HARD BOILED EGGS

Place eggs in pan of water. Heat until boiling. Reduce heat and slowly boil for 10 to 15 minutes.
Or
Place eggs in pan of water and bring to a full rolling boil. Cover with lid and turn off stove. Leave in water at least 20 minutes. This is convenient if you have to leave. Just remember to turn off stove and cover pan. When you return - eggs are ready.

DEVILED EGGS

Hardboiled eggs   **Mayonnaise**
Salt   **Pickle relish**

1. Peel eggs and cut in half lengthwise. Scoop out yolk carefully so as not to tear whites.
2. Place all yokes in dish and mash with a fork. Add salt to your taste, enough mayonnaise to give it a soft consistency. Add pickle relish and some of the sweet pickle syrup. This will also make yolks thinner so go carefully with mayonnaise.
3. Refill egg whites. A sprinkle of paprika on top of each will add a little color.

A small pin hole in the end of egg shell will prevent it from cracking while cooking.

GRILLED CHEESE SANDWICHES

1 slice American cheese   Mayonnaise
2 pieces of bread   Margarine

1. Spread bread lightly with mayonnaise.
2. Place one slice of cheese between the pieces of bread.
3. Spread margarine on outside of bread and place in frying pan on medium to medium high temperature.
4. Brown both sides. Mash down lightly with spatula as it is cooking.

1 sandwich

FANCY HOTDOGS

Weiners   Cheese
Bacon   Pickle relish

1. Cut slice in weiner lengthwise.
2. Place strip of cheese and a little sweet relish in opening.
3. Wind strip of bacon around weiner securing at both ends with toothpick.
4. Place in oven and broil on top shelf in electric oven and broiler shelf under flame in gas oven. Watch, it does not take long to cook.

DEVILED HAM SANDWICHES

1 2¼ ounce can deviled ham   1 tablespoon mayonnaise
1 hard boiled egg   2 teaspoons pickle relish

1. Combine ham, chopped egg, a little pickle relish and mayonnaise.
2. Spread mayonnaise on bread and cover with a thick layer of ham.

Makes 2 to 3 sandwiches

TUNA FISH SALAD SANDWICH

See Tuna Salad on page 16. Just spread bread with mayonnaise and a thick layer of salad.

BACON, LETTUCE, AND TOMATO

Easiest and quickest way is to keep a jar of precooked bacon chips and you can make a sandwich any time in minutes. (Found in small jar near salad dressing — Bacos-Bacon Bits) Spread mayonnaise on bread, use leaf or two of lettuce, and a thin slice of tomato. Sprinkle with bacon chips or fry your own.

EGG McSANDWICH

English Muffin or bread   **Bacon, fried**
Egg, fried or scrambled   **Cheese**

Place cooked egg on bread or muffin, top with cheese and bacon.

EGG SALAD SANDWICHES

2 hard boiled eggs   **Sweet pickle relish (optional)**
2 tablespoons mayonnaise   **Salt to taste**

1. Peel eggs and place in a bowl. Mash with a fork until in very small pieces (really squash 'em).
2. Add salt, mayonnaise, and pickle relish and mix well.

We use more sweet syrup from the relish than we do pickles. Use enough mayonnaise to make it thin enough to spread on bread. Allow 1 egg per sandwich.

Meats

MEATS

Baked Ham Slices..51
Brown Gravy..47
Charcoal Steak for 2 48
Chicken Bake 54
Chicken Parmesan 54
Easy Spaghetti I..44
Easy Stroganoff 46
Fried Steaks 47
Fried Venison Steaks 53
Lasagna..49
Meal-In-One Dish 50
Meat Loaf 48
Out Door Beef Kabobs.......................................51
Pork Chop Casserole 52
Rations 43
Salisbury Steak and Gravy 43
Spaghetti II 45
Steak or Beef Casserole 46
Sweet 'n Sour Dinner 45
Weiners and Potato Casserole 52
Wild Duck Breast 53

SEAFOOD
Baked Shrimp in Garlic Butter 56
Boiled Shrimp in Beer.......................................57
Boiled Shrimp II 57
Great Baked Fish 58
Southern Baked Fish Fillets 59
Tuna Casserole...60

SALISBURY STEAK AND GRAVY
The quick and easy version

1 **pound ground meat**
1 **teaspoon salt**
1 **tablespoon margarine**

1 **10½ ounce can cream of mushroom soup**

1. Add salt to meat and mold into 4 or 5 patties.
2. Melt margarine in frying pan, add patties and cook over medium heat 5 or 6 minutes on each side.
3. Spoon off any excess grease that cooks out of meat.
4. Reduce heat and pour can of soup into pan over meat. Let simmer a few minutes to get meat flavor into soup or it will taste just like a can of soup.

If it gets a little thick while you are cooking, you add just a little water to thin, stir and serve hot. Fix rice for the gravy and you are in business.

RATIONS
Ground Meat Casserole

1 **pound ground meat**
1 **medium onion, chopped or**
  ½ cup chopped, frozen
Salt

1 **10½ ounce can cream of tomato soup**
2 **cups instant rice**

1. Bring 2 cups of water to a boil in sauce pan, add ½ teaspoon salt, 2 cups instant rice, stir, let return to a boil, cover and set off heat for 10 minutes.
2. Place ground meat, 1 teaspoon salt, and chopped onion in frying pan on medium to medium high heat.
3. Cook until meat has turned brown. Stir while cooking to make sure all is browned and broken into small pieces - no big lumps.
4. Drain off all the grease.
5. Turn oven on to 350 degrees.
6. In a 8 x 8 inch pan, loaf pan, or casserole dish put half of the rice, then a layer of ground meat and then layer of soup. Repeat a layer of rice, ground meat, and soup.
7. Place in oven at 350 degrees until hot, about 15 to 20 minutes.

EASY SPAGHETTI I

1 **pound ground meat**
2 **tablespoons oil or margarine**
Salt

1 **15 ounce jar prepared**
   spaghetti sauce
1 **8 ounce package spaghetti**

1. Pour oil or margarine in frying pan and heat.
2. Add ground meat and brown, breaking into small pieces. Keep moving the meat around so all will brown.
3. Drain off grease and add jar of prepared spaghetti sauce and mix. Turn heat to low to keep warm until ready to serve.
4. **Noodles:** Boil 5 to 6 cups of water in a deep pan. Add teaspoon of salt and spaghetti noodles. (Be sure water is boiling.)
5. When it returns to a boil, lower heat and cook for 10 to 12 minutes. (Watch it will boil over if you are not careful.)
6. Drain - Place noodles on individual plates and add sauce to top.
7. Parmesan cheese sprinkled on top adds a lot.

Note - Be sure water is boiling before adding noodles. One of us put noodles in water before boiling and left them while the sauce cooked. Don't make that mistake.

Serves 2 to 4

SPAGHETTI II

1 pound ground meat
2 tablespoons oil
½ teaspoon salt
1 onion, chopped
1 bell pepper, chopped
1 4 ounce can mushroom,
   pieces

1 16 ounce can tomatoes
1 6 ounce can tomato paste
1 8 ounce package spaghetti
   noodles
Water
Optional - bay leaves, ½
   teaspoon oregano

1. Pour vegetable oil or margarine into large frying pan on medium to medium high heat. Lightly brown onion and bell pepper.
2. Add ground meat and salt. Cook until brown, stirring and breaking into small pieces. Drain off grease.
3. Pour in tomatoes, (breaking into small pieces). Add the can of mushrooms, tomato paste and two tomato paste cans filled with water (12 ounces).
4. Add other spices if you desire.
5. Lower heat to just simmering and cook 1 hour. If gets too thick add a little more water.
6. Noodles - See Easy Spaghetti page 44.

Serves 4

SWEET 'N SOUR DINNER

½ pound ground meat
Egg noodles or rice
1 tablespoon margarine

1 3 ounce jar sweet and sour
   sauce

1. Roll ground meat into small balls.
2. Melt margarine in small frying pan on medium to medium high heat.
3. Add meat balls and brown.
4. Pour off grease, add sweet and sour sauce and heat.
5. Cook noodles or rice according to directions on package.
6. Place noodles or rice on plate and top with meat and sauce.

Serves 2

EASY STROGANOFF

1 pound ground meat
1 10½ ounce can cream of
   mushroom soup

½ pint sour cream (8 ounces)
Salt
8 ounce package of noodles

1. Place meat in frying pan on medium to medium high heat. Cook, stirring and breaking meat into small pieces until all is browned.
2. Pour grease off (in a can, not sink).
3. Add mushroom soup and sour cream stirring to mix evenly with meat. Reduce heat and keep warm until serving time.
4. Boil 6 to 8 cups of water in a large pan. Add salt as noodle package directs.
5. Add noodles, bring back to a boil, reduce heat, slowly boil 10 to 12 minutes. Be sure to watch - will boil over if too high - not boil at all if too low.
6. Drain noodles, serve on plates and spoon meat mixture on top.

STEAK OR BEEF CASSEROLE
"Easy to prepare - just takes a long time to cook"

1½ pounds round or chuck
   steak
1 10½ ounce can cream of
mushroom soup

2 teaspoons dry onion soup
   mix
¼ cup cooking wine

1. Turn oven on to 300 degrees.
2. Cut steak into bite size pieces (do not brown meat).
3. Combine all the ingredients in a casserole dish or pan and cover with foil.
4. Bake at 300 degrees for 4 hours.
5. Serve over rice or noodles.

This recipe can easily be doubled.

FRIED STEAKS

2 or 3 cubed steaks   **Milk**
Flour   **3 or 4 tablespoons cooking oil**
Salt and pepper

1. Put oil in frying pan and heat on medium high.
2. Salt and pepper meat.
3. Pour ¼ to ½ cup milk in small bowl and spoon 3 or 4 tablespoons of flour in a saucer or dish.
4. Dip each steak into milk and then into flour, getting flour on both sides.
5. Place in hot grease and cook over medium to medium high heat 3 to 4 minutes on each side.

Our grandmother's cook called this chicken fried steak. She had a thick crust by first dipping into the flour, then the milk and back into the flour. Either way easy and good. It is real easy to make brown gravy for your rice or potatoes after frying steak. Check out the recipe below.

BROWN GRAVY

2 or 3 tablespoons of drippings   **1 cup milk**
**   or cooking oil**   **Salt and pepper**
2 to 3 tablespoons flour

1. Save 2 or 3 tablespoons of grease from cooking meat. If it is burned or too crisp - wipe out frying pan and start with cooking oil.
2. Heat oil and add flour, stirring continuously. This will become pasty - continue to cook and stir until brown.
3. Slowly add milk, stirring vigorously to mix evenly. If too thick add a little more milk.
4. Add salt and pepper to taste.

Lots of pepper makes for super brown gravy. We really add a lot.

CHARCOAL STEAK FOR 2

1½ pounds sirloin steak ¾ to 1   1 tablespoon meat tenderizer
    inch thick   for each cup of dressing
1 cup Italian dressing

1. Cut steak into pieces about 3 x 3 inches - removing all of the fat. Place pieces in a bowl.
2. Combine salad dressing and meat tenderizer. Pour over meat and marinate for about 1 hour.
3. Cook on grill - turn every few minutes - Baste with remaining marinade.
4. Cut into steak to check for desired doneness.

Also good for grilling venison steaks.

MEAT LOAF

2 pounds ground meat   2 teaspoons salt
1 cup of crushed corn flakes   ½ to 1 teaspoon pepper
    cereal or dry bread crumbs   2 eggs
1 medium size onion, chopped   2 or 3 strips bacon (optional)
1 8 ounce can tomato sauce

1. Turn oven on to 350 degrees.
2. Break eggs into a small bowl and beat lightly with fork - just enough to mix.
3. In a large bowl combine meat, crumbs, onion, seasoning, eggs and all but 2 or 3 tablespoons of tomato sauce.
4. Mix well and put into a loaf pan or mold into a loaf not too tall and place in baking pan.
5. Lay strips of bacon on top and bake in preheated oven 1 to 1¼ hours.
6. Remove from pan with a spatula and spoon remaining tomato sauce over top.

Recipe can be cut in half - but leftovers make great sandwiches.

Serves 6 to 8

LASAGNA
"Great for company"

1 pound ground meat
1 15 ounce jar spaghetti sauce
   (spicy)
8 to 10 lasagna noodles

½ pound or 5 to 6 slices of
   Mozzarella cheese
12 ounce carton cottage
   cheese
Parmesan cheese

1. Turn oven on at 350 degrees to preheat.
2. Brown meat in a large frying pan over medium high heat. Stir to make sure all is browned and broken into small pieces - no big lumps.
3. Drain off grease that has cooked out of meat. (Tilt pan and dip out all you can - you want the taste of meat, not grease.)
4. Add jar of spaghetti sauce.
5. Cook noodles in a large pan. (Directions on package. You just boil the water, add salt, vegetable oil and noodles and cook 12 to 15 minutes.) Drain noodles.
6. Spread vegetable oil or margarine on sides and bottom of a 9 x 13 inch casserole dish.
7. Place a layer of noodles flat on bottom of dish or pan, then a layer of spaghetti sauce, mozzarella cheese, cottage cheese and parmesan cheese, then second layer of noodles, sauce, mozzarella, cottage cheese and parmesan.
8. Bake in preheated oven for 30 minutes.
9. Take out of oven and let set 5 to 10 minutes. It needs this extra time to "set up" otherwise it is a little too runny.

Serves 6

MEAL-IN-ONE-DISH
"Great for Entertaining"

1 cup uncooked macaroni	1 small onion chopped or
1 teaspoon salt	chopped, frozen onion
1½ to 2 pounds ground meat	1 16 ounce can whole kernel
1 10½ ounce can mushroom	corn
soup	1 16 ounce can small English
1 10½ ounce can cream of	peas
tomato soup	1 8 ounce can tomato sauce
	1 cup grated cheddar cheese

1. Using a deep pan, bring 6 cups of water to a boil and add 1 teaspoon salt. Pour in macaroni, return to a boil, reduce heat and cook for 10 minutes.
2. Drain off water and pour macaroni into a large mixing bowl or pan.
3. While macaroni is boiling cook meat and onions. First, spray frying pan with non-stick spray or use a little cooking oil or a tablespoon of margarine. Add meat and onions and brown, breaking meat lumps down into small pieces.
4. Drain off grease and add meat and onions to macaroni.
5. Pour the rest of the ingredients into bowl; the tomato and mushroom soups, tomato sauce, and the drained peas and corn.
6. Fold it all together getting it as evenly mixed as possible.
7. Now turn it into a large casserole dish and cover top with grated cheese.
8. Bake at 350 degrees until bubbly and hot all the way through. Serve with salad - a complete meal.

This is great for company. You can prepare ahead, clean kitchen up, and just slide casserole into heated oven 20 to 30 minutes before serving time. For company use large casserole 13½ x 8½. Serves 8 to 10. For several meals use 2 or more smaller casseroles, top each with grated cheese but bake only what you need now. Cover the others tightly with foil and freeze. Set out to thaw 4 to 5 hours and heat through at serving time.

OUT DOOR BEEF KABOBS

Steak   **Onions**
Italian salad dressing   **Bell peppers**
Tomatoes   **Mushrooms**

1. Cut steak into small cubes and marinate in Italian salad dressing. (Put meat in deep bowl, pour salad dressing over it and place in refrigerator overnight or at room temperature 2 or 3 hours.)
2. Stir and turn meat several times to get ones on top in marinade.
3. Place on skewers with vegetables and cook over grill.

Vegetables -

Cut in large enough pieces not to fall apart while cooking. Small patio tomatoes or salad tomatoes are perfect. You skewer the whole tomato. Cut onions lengthwise in 4 to 6 pieces so skewer will go through all layers, not in slices or rings.

BAKED HAM SLICES

1 large ham slice   **Milk**

1. Turn oven on to 350 degrees.
2. Cut several slashes in outer edges through fat into the meat to prevent sides curling up when it shrinks while cooking.
3. Place in glass baking dish or pan and pour milk over ham until it just covers top.
4. Bake uncovered at 350 degrees for 30 minutes.
5. Remove from milk and serve.

Milk makes it more tender and takes out a lot of the salt.

Serves 2 or 3

PORK CHOP CASSEROLE
You can cut this recipe in half

4 to 6 pork chops
2 to 4 tablespoons of vegetable
  oil or margarine
1 package dry onion soup mix

3 cups of hot water
1 cup long grain rice (not
  instant)

1. Turn oven on to preheat to 350 degrees.
2. Heat oil in frying pan.
3. Place chops in hot oil and brown on both sides then remove from pan.
4. Spread uncooked rice in a large shallow baking pan or casserole dish.
5. Sprinkle dry onion soup mix over the rice and then place chops on top of this.
6. Add hot water to pan and cover it tightly with foil.
7. Bake at 350 for 40 minutes.

WEINERS AND POTATO CASSEROLE

6 to 8 weiners   Frozen hash brown potatoes

1. Turn oven on to 400 degrees.
2. Thaw hash browns and slice weiners crosswise.
3. Grease the side and bottom of casserole dish.
4. Make a layer of potatoes, then a layer of weiner slices, a layer of potatoes, a layer of weiner slices and end with a layer of potatoes.
5. Cover casserole with foil and bake in the 400 degree oven for 25 minutes.
6. Remove foil and cook uncovered for 10 minutes.

Serves 4 to 6

FRIED VENISON STEAKS

Venison steaks   **Milk**
Flour   **Cooking oil**

1. Beat steaks on both sides with meat hammer, coke bottle or something heavy (we are not responsible for broken glass in steak - so - just go buy a meat hammer).
2. Heat oil in frying pan on medium heat.
3. **Rees' version** - After beating steak, salt and pepper them, dip into milk and then into flour for a crust and fry on both sides.
3. **Mark's version** - After beating steaks, place steaks in frying pan without flour and fry. Do not salt until through cooking.
4. We both put steaks when fried in pan with a very small amount of water, cover pan with foil and place in oven at 300 to 325 degrees to steam until ready to eat. This makes steaks tender. It is best to put steaks on wire rack or on trivet to be above water to steam but if you do not have one it is fine.

WILD DUCK BREAST

4 wood duck breasts   **Garlic powder**
Zesty Italian salad dressing **Lemon juice**
Salt and pepper   **Worcestershire sauce**
½ teaspoon minced onion   **Bacon strips**

1. Place ducks in bowl.
2. Sprinkle each breast with a little lemon juice, a shake or two of garlic powder, pepper, and a little salt.
3. Pour Italian dressing over birds and let marinate 3 to 4 hours.
4. Turn oven on to 400 degrees.
5. Place ducks in baking dish or pan. Lay a strip or two of bacon across each breast. Pour in just enough marinade to steam them, about ¼ inch, then add a little Worcestershire.
6. Cover tightly with foil and bake at 400 degrees for 1½ hours.

Recipe the same for whole ducks - we just cook the breast because that is all the meat on a wood duck.

CHICKEN BAKE
"So easy"

1 chicken, cut-up or 8 to 10
   pieces you like
1 envelope dry onion soup mix

1 8 ounce bottle French Salad
   Dressing

1. Turn oven on to 350 degrees to preheat.
2. Put chicken pieces in flat bottom baking dish or pan.
3. Combine salad dressing and soup mix and pour over chicken pieces.
4. Bake in oven uncovered for 1½ hours.

CHICKEN PARMESAN
Great for that date

4 boned chicken breast halves
Salt and pepper
½ stick margarine, melted

½ cup grated Parmesan cheese
½ cup cracker crumbs

We buy chicken breasts and cut the bones and ribs out. It is a lot cheaper and not difficult to do but you can buy boned breasts or you can leave the bones in.

1. Season chicken with salt and pepper.
2. Dip into melted margarine and then into a mixture of half and half Parmesan and crumbs. (We use seasoned crumbs - found with stuffing mix, croutons, etc. in a grocery store, comes in a shaker like the Parmesan cheese.)
3. If using boned breast, roll breast up - place in a baking dish - seam side down.
4. Bake at 350 degrees for 35 to 45 minutes.

   We serve these on top of a plate of yellow rice. Not only looks impressive - it taste great. You can fix them ahead of time and put in refrigerator. 45 minutes to 1 hour before serving time place in preheated oven.

Seafood

BAKED SHRIMP IN GARLIC BUTTER
"Terrific"

1 pound raw shrimp
½ stick of butter or margarine
¼ cup cooking oil
1 clove garlic, crushed or ½
   teaspoon garlic powder

2 tablespoons lemon juice
½ teaspoon salt
Dash of cayenne pepper
2 tablespoons chopped parsley

1. Turn oven on bake and set temperature at 400 degrees to preheat.
2. Rinse shrimp, remove shells leaving tails on. Wash under cold running water. Drain; pat dry.
3. Melt butter in 13 x 9 x 2 inch baking dish or pan.
4. Add oil, parsley, garlic, salt, cayenne, and lemon juice; mix well.
5. Add shrimp and carefully stir in butter to make sure all are coated.
6. Bake at 400 degrees for 9 to 12 minutes.
7. Using tongs, remove shrimp to platter. Pour garlic mixture over all or serve in a pitcher to be poured by individuals.

Recipe can easily be doubled.

Serves 2 to 3.

BOILED SHRIMP IN BEER

2 pounds shrimp
1½ cans of beer
1 onion, sliced

2 stalks celery
1 tablespoon salt

1. Wash shrimp in cold water.
2. Put beer, shrimp, onion, celery, and salt in a large pot and bring to a boil.
3. Cook for 5 minutes. Shrimp will turn pink.
4. Set off and let stand until finished cooking (5 to 10 minutes). Just taste one every minute or 2. Do not let over cook.

BOILED SHRIMP II

Shrimp
Water

Shrimp and crab boiling spices
Salt

Shrimp and crab boiling spices are sold in boxes at grocery stores and seafood markets. One seen in our area is Crab Boil. Use the amount of water and spices recommended by your particular brand.

1. Bring water to a boil.
2. Add bag of spices or amount shown on package directions.
3. Add shrimp and let return to a boil.
4. Reduce heat and cook for 5 minutes. Shrimp will turn pink and pull away from the back of the shell. Do not over cook.
5. Remove from heat and let stand in water 10 minutes to finish cooking and absorb spices.
6. Drain - rinse in cold water and serve.

See recipe for cocktail sauce.

GREAT BAKED FISH
"A Little Trouble - But Great!"

4 to 5 pounds of fish - whole
1½ sticks margarine
¾ cup chopped onion
¾ cup chopped celery
½ teaspoon garlic powder

1 8 ounce can tomato sauce
1 teaspoon sugar
Squirt of Worcestershire sauce
⅓ cup white wine

Sauce
1. Melt margarine at medium heat in a small sauce pan.
2. Add onion, celery, tomato sauce, garlic, sugar and Worcestershire sauce.
3. Cook on very low heat (so that it just barely simmers) for at least 45 minutes.

Baking
1. Preheat oven to 300 degrees.
2. Salt and pepper fish inside and out and place in a baking dish or pan.
3. Pour wine over fish and then pour on cooked sauce.
4. Bake uncovered in a 300 degree oven for 1 hour.

You can prepare the sauce ahead of time. Mom use to cook the sauce and send it back to school with me so I could bake and share my weekend catch with my fraternity buddies.

SOUTHERN BAKED FISH FILLETS
Bass, Red Snapper, Grouper

Boned, skinned fillets
Salt and pepper
Butter

Diced onion
Canned evaporated milk

Use fillets of any thick fish.

1. Salt and pepper fish.
2. Grease a baking dish and completely fill the dish with fish. Place pieces close together. It is absolutely necessary to fill the entire dish so use a dish just barely large enough.
3. Place pats of butter on each piece and cover with diced onions.
4. Pour evaporated milk over all; just enough to come to the top of the onions, but not enough to float them.
5. Bake at 350 degrees for 1½ hours until golden brown and moisture is baked out. Baste occasionally (dip milk over fish tops).

The amount of each of the ingredients just depends on the number of fillets and size of dish.

TUNA CASSEROLE

1 6½ ounce can tuna
1 8½ ounce can green peas
1 10½ ounce can cream of
   mushroom soup

½ cup milk
1 cup potato chips, crumbled
½ 8 ounce package of noodles

1. Turn oven on to 350 degrees to preheat.
2. Boil 6 to 8 cups of water in a large sauce pan, then add noodles, reduce heat and boil 10 to 12 minutes.
3. While noodles are cooking drain tuna and break into flakes.
4. Combine flaked tuna, peas, mushroom soup and milk.
5. Grease the bottom and sides of a casserole dish with a little oil.
6. Drain noodles when done.
7. Place a layer of noodles in dish, then a layer of tuna mixture, another layer of noodles and layer of mixture.
8. Crumble potato chips all over top and place in the preheated oven. Bake for 30 minutes.

Serves 4

Vegetables

VEGETABLES

Baked Corn on the Cob 68
Baked Potato Deluxe 69
Baked Potatoes 69
Boiled Corn on the Cob 68
Boiled Potatoes 70
Broccoli Casserole 64
Brown Rice 73
Cabbage..65
Cauliflower and Cheese 67
Cheese Grits 71
Corn Casserole 68
Corn on the Cob 68
Delicious Baked Beans 63
English Peas Deluxe......................................66
French Fries...70
Fresh Broccoli 64
Glazed Carrots 65
Green Bean Casserole 63
Green Peas In Sauce 66
Homemade Macaroni and Cheese 72
Instant Rice 73
Macaroni and Cheese......................................72
Mashed Potatoes 70
Packaged Macaroni and Cheese 72
Regular Rice 73
Scalloped Potatoes 71
Squash Casserole 74

GREEN BEAN CASSEROLE

2 16 ounce cans French style green beans

1 10½ ounce can cream mushroom soup
1 can fried onion rings

1. Drain water from beans.
2. Combine beans, soup and ½ of fried onion rings and pour into casserole dish.
3. Bake at 350 degrees for 15 minutes.
4. Sprinkle remaining onions over top. Return to oven for 5 to 10 minutes.

You can cut this recipe in half - just mix 1 can of beans with ½ can of soup. Mix the other ½ with milk and use it the way it was meant - as a cup of soup.

DELICIOUS BAKED BEANS

1 32 ounce can pork and beans
½ cup brown sugar
1 small onion, chopped (or 1 cup frozen chopped onion)

1 or 2 globs of catsup
1 jerk of Worcestershire sauce
2 or 3 strips of bacon

1. Pour beans in glass casserole or pan.
2. Add onions, sugar, catsup and Worcestershire sauce. Stir to mix it all together.
3. Lay uncooked bacon strips on top. Cover tightly with aluminum foil and bake in an oven preheated to 400 degrees for 30 to 40 minutes.
4. Remove foil and bake 20 to 30 minutes longer to thicken.

This is the best way, but if you are short on time you can reduce covered cooking time. If you are in a hurry just cook uncovered at 350 degrees for 45 minutes to 1 hour.

Our cousin, Bill adds weiners, cut in small pieces to his beans. Makes a good addition. Everyone at the hunting club loves them. Try it for a change.

BROCCOLI CASSEROLE
"A real favorite"

2 10 ounce packages frozen
   chopped broccoli
1 teaspoon salt
1 cup cooked rice

1 8 ounce jar Cheez Whiz
   cheese spread
1 10½ ounce can cream
   chicken soup

1. Bring 1 to 1½ cups of water with 1 teaspoon salt to a boil. Add broccoli, return to a boil, reduce heat and cook 8 to 10 minutes.
2. While broccoli is cooking prepare your rice. Place ½ cup of water in a saucepan and bring to a boil. Add ½ cup instant rice, stir, cover with a lid and set aside until water is absorbed.
3. Remove broccoli from stove and drain off water.
4. Add cheese while broccoli is hot. Stir to melt it and mix evenly.
5. Add chicken soup and rice, mix well and pour into a casserole dish or 8 x 8 pan.
6. Just before serving time place in a 350 degree oven until heated through.

This can be prepared earlier in day for company or even the day before and refrigerated. Just allow more time to heat before serving.

Serves 6 to 8

FRESH BROCCOLI

1 bunch broccoli
1 teaspoon salt

2 tablespoons margarine or
   butter

1. Wash broccoli under running water and remove any remaining leaves. Cut dry end from stalk and peel off outer layer of stalk if tough.
2. Place in small amount of water, about a cup, add salt and bring to a boil.
3. Reduce heat and cook for 15 minutes.
4. Remove from water to dish and top with butter. Ready to eat.

CABBAGE

1 small head of cabbage   Salt and pepper
2 beef bouillon cubes   Water

1. Remove outer leaves and cut out stem; discard.
2. Cut cabbage (Some cut head into quarters but we like ours cut up more. We slice it in 2 or 3 inch strips.)
3. Put bouillon cubes in boiling water, add 1 or 2 teaspoons of salt. Place cabbage in water and cook until tender. About 10 to 15 minutes.
4. Drain - add pepper to taste.

GLAZED CARROTS

1 16 ounce can carrots   2 tablespoons brown sugar
1 to 2 tablespoons margarine

1. Heat carrots in saucepan.
2. Pour off liquid and add margarine and brown sugar.
3. Carefully turn to make sure all carrots are coated with sugar. You can use sliced or the tiny whole carrots. We like the whole ones.

Serves 3 to 4

GREEN PEAS IN SAUCE

1 16 ounce can English peas   **1 10½ ounce can cream of
                                        mushroom soup**

1. Drain water from peas and pour into saucepan.
2. Add soup and heat. Do not let it boil.

Nothing fancy but it's better than just dumping out a can of peas.

ENGLISH PEAS DELUXE

**1 16 ounce can tiny English
    peas**
2 eggs, hard boiled

**1 10½ ounce can cream of
    mushroom soup**
1 2 ounce jar pimento pieces
1 cup potato chips

1. Turn oven on to 325 degrees to preheat.
2. Drain water from peas and pimento, and slice the hard boiled
   eggs.
3. Grease the bottom and sides of a casserole dish with margarine.
4. Combine peas, pimento, eggs and soup in a bowl and gently mix.
5. Pour into greased dish, top with crumbled potato chips and bake
   325 degrees 25 to 30 minutes.

Serves 4

CAULIFLOWER AND CHEESE

½ head of fresh cauliflower
½ teaspoon salt
2 cups water

4 tablespoons mayonnaise
½ cup grated or shredded
   cheese
1 teaspoon prepared mustard

1. Turn oven on to 375 degrees to preheat.
2. Remove outer green leaves from cauliflower and wash under running water.
3. In a saucepan, on top of the stove bring water to a boil, add salt and cauliflower, cover, reduce heat and slowly boil for 15 minutes.
4. Carefully - remove cauliflower to a baking dish (use a flat spatula to keep it from breaking up).
5. Mix mayonnaise, mustard, and cheese together and spread over the cauliflower.
6. Place in preheated oven for 10 minutes.

This can be prepared in advance. You can cook cauliflower - remove to baking dish, spread with cheese mixture and then set aside. Just before serving slide into your heated oven for 10 to 15 minutes - makes it a good dish for company since you can prepare it ahead of time.

CORN ON THE COB

Use fresh corn. The shorter the length of time from "picking to eating" the better. Corn found at farmers markets, pulled that day will be more tender and juicy. Frozen corn on the cob is surprisingly good and available all year.

BOILED CORN ON THE COB

1. Remove outer husk, try to remove the silks (a brush helps) and cut out any bad spots.
2. Drop ears into boiling water for 6 to 12 minutes.
3. Remove from water. Spread with butter and salt.

BAKED CORN ON THE COB
"Roasting Ears" Delicious and extra tender

1. Remove husk and silks as for boiled corn.
2. Coat each ear with butter and sprinkle with salt and pepper.
3. Roll each ear in foil and place in 400 degree oven.
4. Roast for 40 minutes to 1 hour.

   Charcoal Grill - can also be baked on grill - 15 to 20 minutes - turn several times.

CORN CASSEROLE

1 16 ounce can cream style corn
1 to 2 tablespoons margarine
1 egg
Salt and pepper
Canned onion rings or potato chips

1. Turn oven on to 350 degrees to preheat.
2. Smear bottom and sides of casserole dish with margarine.
3. Beat egg and mix with corn, margarine and seasoning.
4. Pour into the greased casserole and top with canned onion rings or crushed potato chips - it will not take but about ½ the can.
5. Bake in a preheated oven at 350 degrees for 30 minutes.

BAKED POTATOES

1. Wash and dry potatoes
2. Rub peel with a little vegetable oil.
3. Place in oven preheated to 400 degrees for 40 to 60 minutes.
4. Remove from oven, cut cross in top and fill with butter. You may want to wrap each potato in foil to bake. This keeps the skin soft.

Microwave
1. Wash and dry potatoes.
2. Prick each potato with 3 or 4 holes.
3. Allow 5 minutes cooking time for each potato.

BAKED POTATO DELUXE

Potatoes   **Milk**
Margarine   **Cheddar cheese**
Salt

1. Wash and dry potatos and rub skins with a little vegetable oil or margarine.
2. Bake potatoes in 400 degree oven for 40 minutes to 1 hour depending on size of potatoes.
3. Remove from oven, cut in half lengthwise. (You will have to grasp them with a towel or hot pad) scoop out potato and place in mixing bowl. (Be careful not to cut or tear peel).
4. Mash potato with 1 or 2 tablespoons margarine and a little salt. Then add a tablespoon or 2 of milk to thin.
5. Scoop back into potato shell and top with cheese.
6. Put back in oven to melt cheese.

Delicious - good looking for company and really not hard - just takes a few extra minutes. You can prepare them ahead of time and put in oven to heat and melt cheese just before serving.

FRENCH FRIES

Potatoes   **Cooking oil**

1. Wash, peel and cut potatoes in thin long pieces.
2. Dry on paper towel (if wet, grease will splatter.)
3. Heat vegetable oil in frying pan. Slowly add potato pieces to grease and fry until golden brown - 7 to 10 minutes.
4. Remove to paper towel, drain and salt.

BOILED POTATOES

1. Peel, rinse, and cut into small pieces.
2. Place in a small pan, cover with water, add a little salt and bring to a boil.
3. Reduce heat and continue to boil for about 10 to 20 minuts. You can tell when they are done by cutting 1 or 2 with a fork. Drain and add margarine.

MASHED POTATOES

2 or 3 potatoes (medium size)   **2 tablespoons milk**
2 to 3 tablespoons margarine   **Salt to taste**

1. Cook the same as for boiled potatoes.
2. Add margarine and mash well with fork (**really well** - to get out big lumps).
3. Add a few tablespoons of milk and continue to mix - you do not want lumpy potatoes.

It is easier to use electric mixer if you have one.

SCALLOPED POTATOES
"Easy Cheese Potatoes"

8 potatoes, medium size
2 onions
1 10½ ounce can cheddar
   cheese soup

1 soup can of milk (1¼ cups)
1 teaspoon salt
½ teaspoon pepper

1. Turn oven on to 350 degrees to preheat.
2. Peel and slice potatoes and onions. Lay both in flat bottom casserole or baking pan and sprinkle with salt and pepper.
3. Mix soup and milk and pour over potatoes and onions.
4. Bake in the preheated oven for 45 minutes.

Good and Easy. Recipe can be cut in half.

CHEESE GRITS
"Great with Seafood"

4 cups water
1 cup instant grits
2 tablespoons margarine

¼ cup milk
4 to 6 ounces sharp cheddar
   cheese

1. Boil water and stir in grits. (Following the amounts according to the directions on your brand package.)
2. Reduce heat, cover and cook - when grits are done add margarine and milk and stir well.
3. Chop cheese in small pieces and add. Stir well to melt cheese.

If too thick add a little more milk. South Georgia special.

Serves 6

71

MACARONI AND CHEESE
"3 choices"

Frozen - just heat container 45 minutes in oven.
Packaged - Boil macaroni - add package mixture and milk and bake.
Homemade - Boil macaroni, add 4 ingredients and bake.

Home made is just as easy, really no more trouble - you just have to buy macaroni, cheese, egg, margarine and milk. They are not all in one box.

PACKAGED MACARONI AND CHEESE

1. Add macaroni to 4 to 6 cups of boiling water, reduce heat and cook 6 to 12 minutes. Drain.
2. Krafts Macaroni and Cheese Deluxe package contains a can of prepared cheese mixture ready to pour over macaroni and bake. Other brands have a package of grated cheese. You sprinkle cheese over macaroni, add milk (usually ¼ cup) and bake in oven 20 minutes at 350 degrees.

HOMEMADE MACARONI AND CHEESE

4 ounces macaroni	2 eggs
4 to 6 ounces of sharp cheddar cheese	2 tablespoons margarine or butter
2 cups milk	

1. Place macaroni in 4 to 6 cups of boiling water. Cook for 6 to 12 minutes and then drain off water.
2. Pour macaroni into a baking dish or pan and add margarine.
3. Cut cheese into small pieces and mix in with the hot macaroni.
4. Put eggs in a small bowl and beat. Add milk, mix well and pour over macaroni and cheese.
5. Bake 30 minutes or until it has set.

INSTANT RICE

Instant rice   **Water**
Salt

Use the same amounts of water and rice.
1. Put water in saucepan on high heat.
2. Add salt according to directions on box.
3. When water boils, add rice, mix well, cover with lid and set off burner. Rice will absorb water - easy and good.

REGULAR RICE

2½ cups water   **1 teaspoon salt**
1 cup rice   **1 tablespoon margarine**

1. Bring water to boil in a saucepan.
2. Add salt, margarine and rice.
3. Cover with lid and reduce heat. Let simmer for 20 minutes.
4. Remove from heat and let set for about 5 minutes longer.

BROWN RICE

1 cup rice (not instant)   **1 10½ ounce can onion soup**
1 10½ ounce can beef   **½ stick margarine**
   consomme soup

1. Turn oven on to 350 degrees.
2. Place margarine in a casserole dish and melt. You can do this on top of the stove or using the oven.
3. Add rice and both soups to melted margarine.
4. Cover with foil and cook in preheated oven for an hour.
5. Remove the cover, stir it all up good and cook it about 15 minutes more without cover.

SQUASH CASSEROLE

8 to 10 yellow squash (2½ to 3 pounds)
1 onion or ½ cup of frozen chopped onion
1 tablespoon sugar
1 to 2 tablespoons salt
1 egg
6 tablespoons margarine
Pepper to taste
Cracker crumbs

1. Wash and cut squash into small slices, discarding end pieces.
2. Place squash, sugar, salt and onion into a pan of water. Not necessary to cover the squash with water. Bring to a boil, reduce heat and slowly boil for 10 to 20 minutes.
3. Remove from heat and drain. Mash squash with a fork and drain again.
4. Add beaten egg and 2 tablespoons margarine, taste and add more salt if necessary and pepper to taste.
5. Place in a greased casserole dish. 8 x 8 or oblong one. Sprinkle with cracker crumbs. Top with thin slices of margarine or melt some and pour over crumbs.
6. Bake in a preheated oven at 350 degrees for 20 to 30 minutes.

You can make a smaller amount but it is good reheated and you can freeze leftovers in small dishes for later meals.

*You can buy cracker crumbs at any grocery store. If you do not have any you can crumble up salad croutons, saltines or oyster crackers.

Desserts

DESSERTS

Alright!! Cake 78
Apple Pie 84
Baking 77
Banana Pudding 90
Butterscotch Treats 89
Cakes 77
Chocolate Chewy 80
Chocolate Chip Delight 91
Chocolate Pie 86
Egg Custard Pie 85
Great Tapioca Pudding 91
Hershey Bar Pie 87
Key Limeade Pie 86
Lemon Meringue Pie 88
Peach Crisp 90
Pecan Pie 87
Pie Crust or Pie Shells 82
Pistachio Cake 79
Pound Cake 81
Sherry Cake 78
Six Layer Cookies 88
Southern Cobbler 89

BAKING
"Don't let cake baking scare you!"

You do not have to be a fantastic cake baker like your mother - and all cakes are not long and complicated like that favorite one she always baked for you. There is a cake you can bake that falls somewhere between "Mother" and the "day old" one on the grocery shelf.

Give it a try!

CAKES
"Three levels to choose from"

1. **The 1-step cakes**
   This is a package cake mix that comes complete with baking pan, mix, and icing. All you have to do is add water and bake. When cake is cooked you spread frosting mix on top. Look for these in your large grocery stores.

2. **The package cake mix**
   These come 1 layer (7½ ounce) box or 2 layer (18½ ounce) size. Different flavors or different brand names may vary slightly but you usually just add water, eggs, mix well, pour into your own pan and bake. You can buy a can of frosting ready to spread on cake usually on the aisle with the cake mixes.

3. **Start with a package mix**
   Add a couple extra ingredients and have a special "homemade cake".

4. **Bake your own from scratch**
   Not hard - you just have to have flour, eggs, milk, sugar, margarine, and vanilla.

77

ALRIGHT!! CAKE

1 yellow cake mix (2 layer size)   1 cup chopped nuts
   18½ ounce   ⅔ box XXXX powdered sugar
1 stick butter   1 8 ounce package cream
3 eggs   cheese

1. Turn oven on to 350 degrees to preheat.
2. Combine cake mix, softened butter, 1 egg and nuts and mix together until crumbly.
3. Pat into a greased 13 x 9 inch pan. (Smear sides and bottom with oil or margarine.)
4. Mix together softened cream cheese, sugar, and the other 2 eggs.
5. Pour over cake mixture in pan and bake at 350 degrees for 40 minutes.
6. Cut into small squares, not over 2 inches, for this is rich.

SHERRY CAKE

1 package yellow cake mix (2   4 eggs
   layer size, 18½ ounces)   ½ cup vegetable oil
1 4 ounce package instant   1 cup sherry (not cooking)
   vanilla pudding   Cinnamon and sugar for pan

Use bundt pan (cake pan with funnel in center).

1. Turn oven on to 350 degrees and grease pan well with shortening and sprinkle entire pan with mixture of ½ sugar and ½ cinnamon. Coat sides well.
2. Combine cake mix, pudding mix, eggs, oil, and sherry in mixer bowl and beat at medium speed for 5 minutes.
3. Pour batter into prepared pan and bake in oven preheated to 350 degrees for 45 minutes or until cake has pulled away from sides of pan. No frosting needed.
4. Turn out of pan - ready to serve.

PISTACHIO CAKE
Easy, Easy and One Great Cake-Moist and Good

1 box white cake mix (2 layer
   size) 18½ ounce
1 3 ounce package pistachio
   instant pudding mix
¾ cup vegetable oil
¾ cup water

4 eggs
½ cup chopped nuts
Glaze
2 tablespoons margarine
½ cup water
½ teaspoon vanilla
2 cups powdered sugar

It is best to use an electric mixer for this. If you do not have one you can use a whisk but be sure to mix well.

1. Turn oven on to 350 degrees.
2. Grease and flour 9 x 12 x 2 inch baking pan (Smear margarine all over bottom and sides of pan. Add 1 or 2 tablespoons of flour to pan and shake it all around so that it sticks to the grease and covers the bottom and sides. Your cake will stick to the pan if you don't.)
3. Put cake and pudding mixes in bowl; add oil, water, and eggs mixing all the time. Beat several minutes.
4. Pour batter into the baking pan and sprinkle the chopped nuts on top.
5. Bake in a preheated oven at 350 degrees for 40 to 45 minutes. Test after 40 minutes, a cake is usually done when you touch the top in the center and it springs back up and also if the cake is pulling away from the sides of the pan.
6. While cake is baking combine in a small mixing bowl - the powdered sugar, water, melted margarine and vanilla. Mix well.
7. When cake is done remove from oven and punch holes over the entire top with a fork (we use a large two prong kitchen fork - it makes nice size holes).
8. Spoon the glaze over the cake allowing it to run down into holes. Pry holes open if necessary to make sure the glaze runs into the cake.

This is really a moist cake and will stay moist for days. The cake is a pretty green. Great for company or a covered dish dinner. You can also use lemon pudding mix.

CHOCOLATE CHEWY
The icing is baked right on the cake

1 3 ounce package chocolate pudding and pie mix

2 cups milk

1 2 layer chocolate cake mix

½ cup chopped pecans

1 cup chocolate chip morsels

1. Turn oven on now so it will be 350 degrees when ready to cook.
2. Grease 9 x 13 inch pan with shortening or margarine. Smear it on bottom and sides.
3. Combine pudding mix and milk in saucepan. Cook over medium heat until thickened, stirring to prevent sticking and burning on bottom.
4. Stir dry cake mix into pudding.
5. Pour into greased cake pan and sprinkle nuts and chocolate chip morsels over top of batter.
6. Place pan in preheated oven. Bake for 30 to 35 minutes.
7. Cut in squares and serve. Great warm.

POUND CAKE

3 sticks of butter or margarine	**2½ cups sifted flour**
6 eggs	**1 teaspoon vanilla**
1 box XXXX sugar	**1 teaspoon lemon extract**

1. Turn oven on to 325 degrees to preheat. Grease and flour pan.*
2. Put softened butter and sugar into the large mixer bowl and beat until well mixed. (This is what recipes mean when they say "cream the butter and sugar".) Beat until light and lemony colored.
3. Add eggs one at a time.
4. Slowly spoon in flour then add vanilla and lemon.
5. Pour into one large tube pan or 2 loaf pans that have been greased and floured.
6. Bake at 325 degrees for 45 minutes to 1 hour. Test by inserting a broom straw, or knife into center - remove slowly. If batter sticks to knife or straw it needs more cooking. If it comes out clean, it is done.
7. Remove from oven and turn upside down on a metal rack or a clean tea towel. After it has cooled a little, remove from pan. Cake should slip out easily, if not run a knife around sides and funnel. I like it just as is with Cool Whip - no need to frost.

* Rub shortening or margarine all over inside of pan. Put in a tablespoon or two of flour, turning and shaking pan so that flour sticks to and lightly covers sides of tube as well as bottom.

This cake can be frozen. We use loaf pans - eat one cake and freeze the other for another day.

PIE CRUST OR PIE SHELLS

They may not taste like your mother's but they are good and easy.

Frozen Pie Crust

1. Set pie shell out 10 to 20 minutes to thaw.
2. Pinch dough all around top between fingers and up off of flat lip of pie pan. This makes it easier to cut and remove from pan without breaking crust. It is now ready for filling with apple, pecan, custard, or ready to bake.

Refrigerator Pie Crust

Comes folded in a box in the dairy department, usually around the canned biscuits, (Already Pie Crust by Pilsbury). You must have your own pie pan, or you can save the ones from frozen crust.

1. Just unfold, place on pie pan, pinch up sides.
2. Ready for filling or for baking.

Baked Pie Shell

Chocolate, lemon, coconut cream, banana cream (any pie with a cooked filling) needs to have a crust already baked before you put in the filling.

1. If frozen shell - set out to thaw.
2. Prick holes with a fork all over sides and bottom. If you do not, air bubbles will form under crust, rise and crack shell.
3. Bake 8 to 10 minuts at 400 degrees or as directed on pie shell.

Graham Cracker Pie Shell

Comes ready made - usually found on grocery shelves near cake mixes and pudding mixes. Use for pies with cooked fillings or frozen fillings such as Cool Whip and ice cream.

Try the Custard Pie — it's always a favorite.

APPLE PIE

2 **frozen pie crusts**
1 **can pie sliced apples or 4 to 5**
  apples
½ **cup sugar**
¼ **cup brown sugar**

¼ **teaspoon salt**
¼ **teaspoon nutmeg**
2 **tablespoons margarine**
½ **teaspoon cinnamon**

1. Turn oven on to 350 degrees to preheat. Remove pie shells from freezer - allow to thaw.
2. Mix sugar, brown sugar, flour, nutmeg, and cinnamon together in a small bowl.
3. If using canned apples, drain and place apples in thawed pie shell. If using fresh apples peel, core, and slice into small pieces and place in shell.
4. Pour dry sugar mixture over apples. Place pats of margarine on top of apples and sugar mixture.
5. Remove second pie crust from pan and lay on top of pie shell with apples. Press crust edges together. (We pinch the bottom crust up off of flat lip of pie pan, so when we remove a piece it will not crumble.) Then cut a lot of slits in top crust.
6. Bake in preheated oven at 350 degrees 30 to 40 minutes.

If you like the open lattice type crust on top instead of solid one just dump out the thawed pie crust on to some waxed paper or counter top and cut into thin strips. Lay strips across pie top. Bake the same.

EGG CUSTARD PIE
"Easy and our favorite"

1 frozen pie shell
3 eggs
2 cups milk

½ teaspoon vanilla
⅓ cup plus 2 tablespoons sugar
Pinch of salt

1. Set pie shell out to thaw 10 to 20 minutes. When soft, pinch top edge of crust up off of the flat lip of the pie pan so it is easier to get out when baked. Set oven at 350 degrees to preheat.
2. Break eggs in medium size bowl and beat just until mixed well. (It goes without saying you throw the shells away.)
3. Add sugar and mix.
4. Add milk, vanilla and salt and beat lightly.
5. Pour into unbaked pie shell. Bake at 350 degrees for 10 minutes -reduce heat to 325 degrees and bake 20 or 30 minutes longer or until it sets and is firm. Test by inserting a knife into center of pie -remove slowly. If custard sticks to knife it needs more cooking.

A lot of times the bottom crust of a custard pie will be soggy. If you put the pie on the bottom shelf for those first 10 minutes and "carefully" move it up to the middle shelf for the remaining time it will bake the bottom faster and prevent "the soggies". Do not forget to reduce heat. This is my favorite! You can use more sugar if you like your custard real sweet, I do not. Some use a whole cup of sugar.

KEY LIMEADE PIE
Quick and easy and no cooking

1 graham cracker pie shell
1 6 ounce can frozen limeade

1 14 ounce can sweetened
   condensed milk
1 9 ounce carton Cool Whip

1. Thaw frozen juice.
2. Pour juice into a bowl, add condensed milk (condensed, not evaporated) and gently stir in Cool Whip.
3. Pour into pie crust and chill in refrigerator until firm.

You may want to save a few tablespoons of the frozen topping mix to spread around top edge of pie for decoration.

This is just as good with lemonade.

CHOCOLATE PIE

1 frozen pie shell
1 3½ ounce box chocolate pie
   and pudding mix

2 cups milk
Cool Whip frozen topping

1. Preheat oven to 400 degrees. Set pie shell out to thaw 10 to 20 minutes. When soft, prick all over the sides and bottom with a fork, be sure to do this to prevent an air bubble forming underneath and ruining your crust. Bake in preheated oven 8 to 10 minutes. Remove and let cool.
2. Put pudding and pie mix in pan and slowly add milk while stirring. (Always stir the liquid into the dry ingredients or you will really have lumps.)
3. Cook on medium heat stirring all the time to keep from sticking. Continue to cook until the pudding comes to a full boil.
4. Set aside to cool a little, about 10 to 15 minutes, and then pour into your baked pie shell. Place in refrigerator to chill.
5. When ready to serve top with frozen topping (set topping out of freezer so it will be soft enough to spread like whipped cream).

HERSHEY BAR PIE
"Super, Delicious and Easy"

1 graham cracker pie shell	18 to 24 marshmallows
6 Hershey bars with almonds	½ cup milk
(1.35 ounce size)	½ 9 ounce tub Cool Whip

1. Place milk, candy bars, and marshmallows in top pan of double boiler and melt (or just use a large pan set in a pan of boiling or simmering water. Chocolate will stick and burn if pan the burner).
2. When melted set out of water to cool - cool complet
3. Fold Cool Whip into the chocolate.
4. Pour into pie crust and chill in refrigerator for at least until ready to serve.

This was our grandmother's recipe. We could tell how because it called for 6 5¢ size Hershey Bars. How long nas it peen since the nickle candy bar?

PECAN PIE
"Easy"

1 frozen pie shell	3 tablespoons margarine,
3 eggs	melted
¾ cup Karo Syrup (white)	1 teaspoon vanilla
¾ cup sugar	1 cup chopped nuts

1. Set pie shell out to thaw (when soft, we pinch top edge of crust up off of the flat lip of the pie pan so it is easier to remove from pan when baked). Set oven at 325 degrees to preheat.
2. Break eggs in medium size bowl and beat enough to mix well.
3. Add sugar, syrup, and vanilla and mix.
4. Pour into thawed pie shell, sprinkle nuts on top and pour melted butter over nuts.
5. Bake at 325 degrees for 1 hour or until mixture is set and firm.

It will rise - touch with finger to see if firm, if not bake a little longer. When you take it out it will settle. Really easy - delicious and will impress everyone.

LEMON MERINGUE PIE

1 frozen pie shell
1 4 ounce box lemon pie and
    pudding mix

2 cups water
1 egg
2 tablespoons sugar

1. Turn oven on to 400 degrees. Set frozen pie shell out to thaw 10 to 20 minutes. When thawed, prick air holes all over bottom and sides with fork, see pie shell instructions. Bake in 400 degree oven 8 to 10 minutes.
2. Empty pudding and pie mix into pan, add water slowly and stir to mix.
3. Separate egg yolk and white. Place egg white in small mixing bowl and use for meringue topping.
4. Break yolk and stir into lemon mix. Cook on medium heat stirring continuously. Bring to a boil and then set aside to cool for about 10 minutes.
5. Pour into baked pie shell. Place egg white in small mixing bowl and beat. Add sugar and continue to beat until stiff (this means when you take out beater the whites will stand in peaks). Spread over lemon filling. Place pie on top shelf in oven and turn to high or broil - Watch closely!! It does not take but a few minutes to start browning. You now have a meringue.

SIX LAYER COOKIES
"Easy, No Mixing"

1 stick margarine
1½ cups graham cracker
    crumbs
1 3½ ounce can flaked coconut

1 cup chopped nuts
1 12 ounce package chocolate
    chips
1 14 ounce can condensed milk

1. Melt margarine in 13 x 9 x 2 inch pan or casserole dish.
2. Sprinkle graham cracker crumbs evenly in bottom of pan on melted margarine.
3. Follow with layer of coconut, layer of chocolate chips and layer of nuts. Pat down each layer.
4. Top with can of condensed milk (not evaporated milk).
5. Bake at 350 degrees for 25 minutes. Cool before cutting. Super!

BUTTERSCOTCH TREATS

1 cup Chinese chow mein
   noodles
1 6 ounce bag of butterscotch
   morsels

½ cup salted peanuts

1. Melt chips in a double boiler (or a regular saucepan set in a larger pan of boiling water).
2. Mix in noodles and nuts.
3. Spoon out small mounds on waxed paper to cool and set.

SOUTHERN COBBLER
Peach - Blueberries - Strawberries
Delicious

1 stick of margarine
1 cup sugar
1 cup Bisquick

1 cup milk
2 cups fruit

1. Turn oven on to preheat to 400 degrees.
2. Melt margarine in glass baking dish or pan - You can do this on top of stove.
3. Combine fruit and sugar and add to margarine in dish.
4. Combine milk and Bisquick and pour over fruit.
5. Place in preheated oven and bake 40 minutes or until crust is done.

You can use frozen fruit - just cut back on the sugar because some is already added. Delicious! If using blueberries, we mash them while stirring in sugar. Blueberry hulls can be a little tough and we like the juice. Either way it is great.

BANANA PUDDING

1 3½ ounce box vanilla pudding mix	1 egg, separated
2 cups milk	Bananas
	Vanilla Waffers

1. Line the bottom and sides of a casserole dish with waffers.
2. Slice banana in thin rounds (peel it first) and place a layer on top of waffers.
3. Combine pudding mix, milk and egg yolk. Break yolk and stir. Cook over medium heat, stirring constantly to prevent sticking. Bring to a boil and then remove from heat.
4. Beat egg white with a handbeater until stiff and will stand in peaks when beater is lifted out. Fold whites into hot pudding. Do not stir it until it is smooth - just barely fold it in.
5. Pour half into bowl, add another layer of bananas and cover with the rest of pudding mix. Cool.

If you have a hard time separating eggs without breaking yolks and getting it in your whites see Tapioca Pudding.

Speedy Method — Use Instant Vanilla Pudding mix. No cooking.

PEACH CRISP
"Or cherry"

1 16 ounce can peach pie filling	1 stick margarine
1 yellow cake mix (1 layer size) 7½ ounces	½ to 1 cup chopped pecans

1. Turn oven on to preheat to 350 degrees.
2. Pour can of pie filling into 8 x 8 inch baking pan.
3. Sprinkle dry cake mix over pie filling.
4. Cut margarine into small slices and lay on top of cake mix.
5. Sprinkle chopped nuts on top.
6. Bake at 350 degrees for 30 to 35 minutes.

Great with ice cream or Cool Whip served on top while warm.

CHOCOLATE CHIP DELIGHT
"Simple - Simple"

Chocolate Chip Cookies   **Cool Whip**

1. Thaw Cool Whip so it is thin and easy to spoon.
1. Use a flat bottom casserole. Line the bottom with layer of cookies.
2. Top cookies with a thick layer of Cool Whip, then a layer of cookies and a layer of Cool Whip. If your dish is deep enough you can make a third layer - just end with a layer of Cool Whip.
3. Put in refrigerator overnight - Best made 18 to 24 hours ahead.

GREAT TAPIOCA PUDDING
"A favorite of ours"

1 3½ ounce box tapioca pudding mix   **2½ cups milk**
      1 egg, separated

1. Separate egg white and yolk and place white in small mixing bowl.
2. Combine pudding mix, milk and egg yolk in a saucepan. Break yolk and mix in well.
3. Cook over medium heat, stirring constantly so it will not stick and burn. Bring to a boil and set off burner.
4. Using a hand beater, beat egg white until stiff and stands in peaks.
5. Fold whites into pudding while it is hot. Do not stir until mixed smooth. Just barely fold in.
6. Pour into 4 individual serving cups.

If you have a hard time separating eggs without breaking yolks and getting it all through your whites, just separate them in your hand. Pour the whole thing in your hand (do wash them) and let the white slide through your fingers.

INDEX

APPETIZERS

Barbeque Bean Dip 10
Chili Dip 9
Cocktail Sauce For Shrimp
   Or Oysters 12
Deviled Ham Dip 11
Dill Dip 10
Fancy Hotdogs 10
Guacamole, Easy............11
Onion Dip 9
Oyster Dip 9
Salmon Spread 11
Shrimp or Oyster
   Cocktails.................12

BREADS

Beer Muffins 23
Biscuits (With Mix) 23
Biscuits, Real 24
Biscuits - 2 Man-Size 23
Cheese Toast 22
Cinnamon Toast 22
Garlic Bread...............22
Muffins, Package 21
Popovers, Grandmother's..24
Rolls, Brown and Serve 21
Rolls, Canned 21

DESSERTS

Cakes

Alright! Cake 78
Chocolate Chewey.........80
Pistachio Cake 79
Pound Cake 81
Sherry Cake 78

Cookies

Butterscotch Treats 89
Six-layer Cookies 88

Pies

Apple Pie 84
Chocolate Pie 86

Pies (Cont.)

Egg Custard Pie 85
Hershey Bar Pie............87
Key Limeade Pie 86
Lemon Meringue Pie.......88
Pecan Pie 87
Pie Crust Or Pie Shells......82

Puddings & Cobblers

Banana Pudding 90
Chocolate Chip Delight 91
Cobbler, Southern 89
Peach Crisp 90
Tapioca Pudding, Great 91

EGGS

Crustless Quiche 34
Cheese And Eggs 36
Deviled Eggs 38
Egg McSandwich 40
Egg Salad Sandwich 40
Eggs, Hard Boiled 38
Fried Eggs 37
Omelettes 35
Sausage and Eggs 36

MEATS

Beef

Beef Kabobs, Out Door 51
Burgers
   Cheeseburgers 28
   Deluxe Hamburger 27
   Mushroom Burger 28
   Old Fashioned
      Hamburger 28
   Onion Burger 29
   Pizza Burger.............29
   Plain Hamburger 27
Chip Beef On Toast,
   Creamed................31
Corned Beef Hash
   And Eggs................31

BEEF (Cont.)

Lasagna .49
Meal-In-One-Dish 50
Meat Loaf 48
Quick Pizza's 29
Rations (Ground Beef
   Casserole). 43
Spaghetti, Easy I 44
Spaghetti II. 45
Steaks
   Charcoal Steak For 2 48
   Salisbury Steak
     And Gravy 43
   Steak, Fried And
     Brown Gravy 47
   Steak Or Beef Casserole . . .46
Stew, Instant 30
Strognoff, Easy. 46
Sweet And Sour Dinner 45

Chicken

Chicken Bake 54
Parmesan Chicken 54

Game

Venison, Fried Steaks. 53
Wild Duck Breast 53

Pork

Ham Slices, Baked 51
Pork Chop Casserole 52

Seafood

Fish, Great Baked 58
Fish, Southern Baked Fillets . .59
Oyster Dip 9
Salmon Spread 11
Shrimp, Baked In
   Garlic Butter 56
Shrimp, Boiled 57
Shrimp, Boiled In Beer 57
Shrimp Or Oyster Cocktail . . .12
Tuna Casserole 60

SEAFOOD (Cont.)

Tuna, Creamed On Toast 30
Tuna Fish Salad Sandwich 35

Weiners

Fancy Hotdogs 34
Weiners And Potato
   Casserole 52

QUICK AND EASY MEALS

Burgers

   Cheeseburgers 28
   Deluxe Hamburgers. 27
   Mushroom Burger 28
   Old Fashioned
     Hamburgers. 28
   Onion Burger 29
   Pizza Burger. 29
   Plain Hamburgers 27
Chip Beef On Toast,
   Creamed. 31
Corned Beef Hash
   And Eggs. 31
Creamed Tuna On Toast. 30
Crustless Quiche 34
Omelettes 35
French Toast 32
Fried Rice 37
Instant Stew 30
Pancakes 32
Quick Pizza's 29

SALADS

Aspic, Quick Salad 18
Banana Salad 17
Congealed Fruit Salad 15
Cranberry Salad 18
Lettuce Wedges 16
Peach Salad 17
Pear Salad 17
Pineapple Salad. 17
Tossed Green Salad 15

SALADS (Cont.)
Tuna Fish Salad 16

SANDWICHES

Bacon, Lettuce, And
    Tomato 40
Deviled Ham Sandwich 39
Egg McSandwich 40
Egg Salad Sandwich 40
Fancy Hotdogs 39
Fried Egg Sandwich 37
Grilled Cheese 39
Tuna Fish Salad Sandwich 40

VEGETABLES

Baked Beans, Delicious 63
Bean Casserole, Green 63
Broccoli Casserole 64
Broccoli, Fresh 64
Cabbage 65
Carrots, Glazed 65
Cauliflower And Cheese 67

VEGETABLES (Cont.)
Corn Casserole 68
Corn On The Cob, Baked 68
Corn On The Cob, Boiled . . . 68
Grits, Cheese 71
Macaroni And Cheese,
    Homemade 72
Macaroni And Cheese,
    Packaged 72
Peas, English Deluxe 66
Peas In Sauce, Green 66
Potato Deluxe, Baked 69
Potatoes, Baked 69
Potatoes, Boiled 70
Potatoes, French Fries 70
Potatoes, Mashed 70
Potatoes, Scalloped 71
Rice, Brown 73
Rice, Instant 73
Rice, Regular 73
Squash Casserole 74

THE BACHELORS COOKBOOK
P.O. Box 117
Waycross, Georgia 31502

Please send me _____ copies of THE BACHELORS COOK-
BOOK at $6.95 plus $1.25 postage and handling, or 3 for
$20.85 plus $2.00 postage. Georgia residents add 4% sales
tax.

Enclosed is my check or money order for $_____

Name _____

Address _____

City _____ State _____ Zip _____

THE BACHELORS COOKBOOK
P.O. Box 117
Waycross, Georgia 31502

Please send me _____ copies of THE BACHELORS COOK-
BOOK at $6.95 plus $1.25 postage and handling, or 3 for
$20.85 plus $2.00 postage. Georgia residents add 4% sales
tax.

Enclosed is my check or money order for $_____

Name _____

Address _____

City _____ State _____ Zip _____

THE BACHELORS COOKBOOK
P.O. Box 117
Waycross, Georgia 31502

Please send me _____ copies of THE BACHELORS COOK-
BOOK at $6.95 plus $1.25 postage and handling, or 3 for
$20.85 plus $2.00 postage. Georgia residents add 4% sales
tax.

Enclosed is my check or money order for $_____

Name _____

Address _____

City _____ State _____ Zip _____

Re-Order Additional Copies

Names and addresses of bookstores, gift shops, etc.
in your area would be appreciated.

_____

_____

_____

_____

_____

_____

Names and addresses of bookstores, gift shops, etc.
in your area would be appreciated.

_____

_____

_____

_____

_____

_____

Names and addresses of bookstores, gift shops, etc.
in your area would be appreciated.

_____

_____

_____

_____

_____

_____